North American Indians Today

North American Indians Today

Apache

Cherokee

Cheyenne

Comanche

Creek

Crow

Huron

Iroquois

Navajo

Ojibwa

Osage

Potawatomi

Pueblo

Seminole

Sioux

North American
Indians Today

Potawatomi

by
Ellyn Sanna

Mason Crest Publishers

Philadelphia

Special thanks to Jones Seel Huyett and the Prairie Band of Potawatomi Indian Nation for their help in creating this book.

Mason Crest Publishers Inc.
370 Reed Road
Broomall, Pennsylvania 19008
(866) MCP-BOOK (toll free)

First printing
1 2 3 4 5 6 7 8 9 10
Library of Congress Cataloging-in-Publication Data on file at the Library of Congress.
ISBN: 1-59084-675-3
1-59084-663-X (series)

Design by Lori Holland.
Composition by Bytheway Publishing Services, Binghamton, New York.
Cover design by Benjamin Stewart.
Printed in the Hashemite Kingdom of Jordan.

Photography courtesy of Jones Seel Huyett. Pictures on pp. 14, 17, 18, 19, 20, 27, and 32 courtesy of the Kansas State Historical Society; picture on p. 69 courtesy of Jack Wooldridge. Picture on p. 6 by Keith Rosco.

Contents

Why is it so important that Indians be brought into the "mainstream" of American life?
I would not know how to interpret this phrase to my people.
The closest I would be able to come would be "a big wide river".
Am I then to tell my people that they are to be thrown into the big, wide river of the United States?

Earl Old Person
Blackfeet Tribal Chairman

Introduction

In the midst of twenty-first-century North America, how do the very first North Americans hold on to their unique cultural identity? At the same time, how do they adjust to the real demands of the modern world? Earl Old Person's quote on the opposite page expresses the difficulty of achieving this balance. Even the common values of the rest of North America—like fitting into the "mainstream"—may seem strange or undesireable to North American Indians. How can these groups of people thrive and prosper in the twenty-first century without losing their traditions, the ways of thinking and living that have been handed down to them by their ancestors? How can they keep from drowning in North America's "big, wide river"?

Thoughts from the Series Consultant

Each of the books in this series was written with the help of Native scholars and tribal leaders from the particular tribe. Based on oral histories as well as written documents, these books describe the current strategies of each Native nation to develop its economy while maintaining strong ties with its culture. As a result, you may find that these books read far differently from other books about Native Americans.

Over the past centuries, Native groups have faced increasing pressure to conform to the wishes of the governments that took their lands. Often brutally inhumane methods were implemented to change Native social systems. These books describe the ways that Native groups refused to be passive recipients of change, even in the face of these past atrocities. Heroic individuals worked to fit external changes into local conditions. This struggle continues today.

The legacy of the past still haunts the psyche of both Native and non-Native people of North America; hopefully, these books will help correct some misunderstandings. And even with the difficulties encountered by past and current Native leaders, Native nations continue to thrive. As this series illustrates, Native populations continue to increase—and they have clearly persevered against incredible odds. North American culture's big, wide river may be deep and cold—but Native Americans are good swimmers!

—Martha McCollough

Breaking Stereotypes

One way that some North Americans may "drown" Native culture is by using stereotypes to think about North American Indians. When we use stereotypes to think about a group of people, we assume things about them because of their race or cultural group. Instead of taking time to understand individual differences and situations, we lump together everyone in a certain group. In reality, though, every person is different. More than two million Native people live in North America, and they are as *diverse* as any other group. Each one is unique.

Even if we try hard to avoid stereotypes, however, it isn't always easy to know what words to use. Should we call the people who are native to North America Native Americans—or American Indians—or just Indians?

The word "Indian" probably comes from a mistake—when Christopher Columbus arrived in the New World, he thought he had reached India, so he called the people he found there Indians. Some people feel it doesn't make much sense to call Native Americans "Indians." (Suppose Columbus had thought he landed in China instead of India; would we today call Native people "Chinese"?) Other scholars disagree; for example, Russell Means, Native politician and activist, claims that the word "Indian" comes from Columbus saying the native people were en Dios—"in God," or naturally spiritual.

Many Canadians use the term "First Nations" to refer to the Native peoples who live there, and people in the United States usually speak of Native Americans. Most Native people we talked to while we were writing these books prefer the simple term "Indian"—or they would rather use the names of their tribes. (We have used the term "North American Indians" for our series to distinguish this group of people from the inhabitants of India.)

Even the definition of what makes a person "Indian" varies. The U.S. government recognizes certain groups as tribal nations (almost 500 in all). Each nation then decides how it will enroll people as members of that tribe. Tribes may require a particular amount of Indian blood, tribal membership of the father or the mother, or other *criteria*. Some enrolled tribal members who are legally "Indian" may not look Native at all; many have blond hair and blue eyes and others have clearly African features. At the same time, there are thousands of Native people whose tribes have not yet been officially recognized by the government.

We have done our best to write books that are as free from stereotypes as possible. But you as the reader also play a part. After reading one of these books, we hope you won't think: "The Cheyenne are all like this" or "Iroquois are all like that." Each person in this world is unique, whatever their culture. Stereotypes shut people's minds—but these books are intended to open your mind. North American Indians today have much wisdom and beauty to offer.

Some people consider American Indians to be a historical topic only, but Indians today are living, contributing members of North American society. The contributions of the various Indian cultures enrich our world—and North America would be a very different place without the Native people who live there. May they never be lost in North America's "big, wide river"!

The Potawatomi's world view is often different from that of the rest of North America.

Chapter 1

An Alternate Value System: Oral Traditions

Boozhoo. Dabindegék!
("Hello. Welcome!" in Potawatomi.)

Long, long ago, when the earth was young, Gitchie Manito, the God of Great Miracles, created the *nIshnabe* (pronounced "nish-nay-bay"). These "original people" first lived along the gulf of the St. Lawrence River, near the Atlantic Ocean, but Gitchie Manito sent a sacred shell, called the *Megis*, to lead them on a journey to the west.

The nIshnabe had three groups, and Gitchie Manito gave them each their own job. The first group was the Ottawa, and they provided food and supplies for the nIshnabe. The second group, the Ojibwa or Chippewa,

A museum model shows how early Potawatomi lived.

kept alive the others' faith in Gitchie Manito. And the third group, the Potawatomi, were the keepers of the fire.

Fire meant life itself to the nishnabe. Without fire they could not cook their food, they could not warm themselves on cold winter nights, and they could not keep away wolves and other dangers that threatened their community. The sacred fire was at the very center of their lives together.

Eventually, each of the three groups settled in a different area around the Great Lakes. When the first white men came to North America, they found the Potawatomi living on the peninsula jutting out into Lake Michigan (where Green Bay, Wisconsin, is today). In the years that followed, the Potawatomi prospered and spread into the land that is now Michigan, Indiana, Illinois, and Ohio.

As the years passed, the Potawatomi kept alive their sense of who they were and from where they came. A few records were kept on birch bark scrolls using *pictographs*, but for the most part, the Potawatomi preserved their stories and culture through oral history. Stories were passed down from generation to generation, linking the past, the present, and the future in a long chain of tradition.

These stories are still important to today's Potawatomi. They give them a sense of who they are in relation to the rest of the world, and they explain the meaning of many aspects of life. Surrounded by the often *invasive* culture of twenty-first-century North America, the Potawatomi rely on their oral traditions to keep them grounded in another *value system*. Stories like the one that follows—about the origin of tobacco—give us all a glimpse into a culture that looks at things differently from the rest of the *Western* world.

Once upon a time, when the Potawatomi still lived near the eastern ocean, an old man named Fox dreamed a strange and marvelous dream about a clearing near his home. He dreamed that something wonderful and extraordinary was about to grow there—and his dream was so powerful that when he woke up he felt compelled to build a fence of fallen trees around the plot of earth.

The other men laughed at him. "How do you expect to grow a garden when you have planted no seeds?" they asked.

Their teasing annoyed Fox so much that he stayed home when the others left for the summer hunt in July. All alone, he tended his field—and when a strange plant sprang up there, he hoed and watered it and waited and wondered.

The old man was friends with a member of the Delaware tribe who lived

Feathers and other objects from the natural world hold spiritual significance for the Potawatomi.

A nineteenth-century photograph of a Potawatomi bark home.

nearby, and when his friend stopped by for a visit, Fox showed him the strange plant that grew in his garden.

"My people have this sacred plant," the Delaware told Fox. "It came to us in a dream, just as it did to you."

"What do you do with the plant?" the old man asked.

The Delaware shook his head. "This plant is a gift from the Creator. He is the one who should show you how to use it."

So Fox decided to *fast* and wait for the Great Spirit to speak to him. When he had gone without food for two days, the Creator appeared to him in a vision. "Gather the leaves," the Great Spirit told him, "and then dry them. These leaves are for prayer. Burn them in the fire as incense. Smoke them in a pipe. Make them your offering at every feast and ceremony. They will carry your spirit to me in prayer."

Fox did as the Creator had told him. His friend the Delaware showed him how to make a pipe from stone and wood. Then Fox waited for the right time to tell the rest of his people about the sacred plant given to him by the Creator.

One day Fox gave a feast and seated the chief on his left. He said to his people, "I have grown a plant in my garden where I planted no seeds. This

Traditional Native Values Vs. Everyday Societal Values

Native Values	Society's Values
emphasis on the group	emphasis on the individual
focus on the present	focus on the future
time is always with us	time is fleeting
age is best	youth is best
cooperation	competition
harmony with nature	nature is there to be used
giving/sharing	taking/saving
aware of the spiritual world	doubts the spiritual world
patience	aggression
religion is all of life	religion is just a piece of life
modesty	self-attention

Adapted from the Jones Seel Huyett's *The Prairie Band Potawatomi: Chapters in Time.*

The Potawatomi are passing along their stories to a new generation.

Potawatomi Value Statement

We the Prairie Band Potawatomi people known as the "Keepers of the Fire" shall:

1. Maintain, protect, and nurture our culture and spiritual and historic values through the celebration of its unique traditions, language, and sovereignty.
2. Promote education as the cornerstone of our values.
3. Show pride and support the endeavors of our youth.
4. Acknowledge, respect, and value the wisdom of our tribal elders with guidance for our future generations.
5. Honor, respect, and strive for justice by treating all with equality and fairness.
6. Protect and maintain tribal lands and other natural resources.
7. Promote, enhance, and sustain the health, safety, and quality of life for all.

A Potawatomi ceremonial dance being performed in the early twentieth century.

Little Chief, a nineteenth-century Potawatomi leader, with his wife and child.

plant is clearly a gift from the Great Spirit, and he has told me in a dream how we are to use the tobacco, this amazing gift. We are to burn it in our fires and smoke it in pipes, and it will carry our prayers to the Creator. I give this feast to celebrate this new blessing that has been given us for all time."

Now the chief stood up and thanked Fox for being faithful to his dreams. "Never forget this man," he told his people, "for he has brought the Creator's gift to us. He will divide the tobacco he has grown among you—take it and use it. Before you go out to hunt, put the tobacco in the fire and tell our Grandfather the fire where you are going and how long you will be gone. Never leave without telling our Grandfather what you are doing and praying to the Creator."

Then Fox showed the people the pipe he had built with the help of his friend the Delaware. Soon everyone had a pipe of wood or stone for smoking tobacco as part of their prayers.

The Potawatomi never used the sacred plant without praying—but when the white men came, they smoked tobacco without understanding its meaning. They smoked it with greed instead of prayer. This was not what the Creator had intended.

Kack-kack, a nineteenth-century Potawatomi chief.

This small boy's name was Ne-kon-we-tak; his picture was taken in the 1870s.

Today, Western culture has made tobacco its own—but the "sacred plant" has lost the meaning it once had for the Potawatomi and other Native people. Tobacco companies get rich from the sale of tobacco—and our society struggles with the ill effects of cigarette addiction. What was given as a gift by the Creator has become a curse for those who die from lung cancer or other diseases related to tobacco abuse.

Today's Potawatomi people must confront this and other issues as they struggle to maintain their traditions in the midst of a conflicting culture.

The loud voices of television and other media come into their homes and sometimes drown out the quiet whisper of their oral traditions. But the Potawatomi are seeking to stay true to their own value system. When they follow the value system that is uniquely theirs, they offer North America an alternative way of looking at things—a way that often leads to health, integrity, and hope.

Today's Potawatomi continue to live out the values of their ancestors.

Chapter 2

A Heritage of Generosity and Loss: Potawatomi History

By the late 1840s, life for the Potawatomi was no longer the same as when they first followed the sacred shell to the west. The white man's coming had changed their lives forever. But even as much of their culture was lost, stories still kept alive their traditions and values. William Mzhickteno, for example, told the story—told to him by his father and other older Potawatomi—of the last buffalo hunt.

The winter ahead promised to be a long and cold one, and so the tribe prepared for a hunt to bring back buffalo to their people. The meat would be cured and preserved, and the hides would be turned into blankets. First, though, before they could leave their *reservation* land, they had to get permits from the *Indian agent*. They were no longer free people who could come and go as they pleased.

When they had their permits, the hunting party, including Mzhickteno's father Joseph and his grandfather Wamego, traveled westward until they found a buffalo herd. The hunters took enough buffalo to get their people through the winter, and then they started home.

On their journey, they came across a small settlement of African Americans who had formed the "town" of Nicodemus—a town that lacked houses and food. The Potawatomi hunters could see that these settlers would not survive the winter. The African Americans had no doubt come to the frontier seeking freedom from the white man's oppression—but the black settlers clearly lacked the experience and knowledge that would get them through the long, bitter winter ahead.

A cradleboard like that used by early Potawatomi.

The buffalo are an important part of Potawatomi history. Today, the Prairie Band Nation has begun their own herd.

That night the Potawatomi hunters sat around their campfire and talked about the Nicodemus settlers. They felt uneasy leaving them to face the winter unprepared—and so they decided to help the settlers build homes like their own.

The next day they rode back to Nicodemus and showed the settlers how to cut slough grass from a nearby creek. Then they taught the African Americans how to build shelters from the grass. But the hunting party still felt uncomfortable leaving the settlers.

"We can't leave them this way," said one of the Potawatomi. "They'll have to have something to eat and skins to wrap themselves in." The Great Spirit moved the hunters to compassion; they decided to give the Nicodemus people half the buffalo they had killed.

When the hunting party finally returned to the reservation, their loads were much lighter than they had expected, but so were their hearts. They were glad they had helped to save a community in trouble—and as the story spread through the reservation, they were remembered as heroes. The generosity demonstrated by the Potawatomi hunting party is all the

Powwows are an opportunity for today's Potawatomi to celebrate cultural unity. They are a modern custom that did not begin until the late nineteenth century.

more remarkable considering that history had treated them no more kindly than it had the black settlers of Nicodemus.

Life had once been good for the Potawatomi. The land in what is today the state of Michigan was rich with resources; everything the people needed came from the forests and lakes or from trade with other tribes. The Potawatomi, like other Native groups, believed that the land belonged to all living things, both human and nonhuman. So long as the Earth's gifts were treated with respect, there would be plenty for everyone.

When white settlers began spreading westward, the Potawatomi failed to understand the concept of land ownership that was so important to European minds. After the birth of the United States, the Potawatomi agreed to sell land to the U.S. government—but they did not grasp what this would mean to them in the years to come.

26 *North American Indians Today*

The 1830 Removal Act was the American government's attempt to send the eastern Indians west of the Mississippi River, leaving the land between the Mississippi and the Appalachian Mountains free for white settlement. Many Indian groups fought to stay in their homelands, but in 1833, the Potawatomi surrendered all their land—about five million acres (2,023,428 hectares)—to the U.S. government. The government promised to pay the Potawatomi tribes for their land, but many of them never received any money.

About a century ago, Eliza Clay Bear with her small granddaughter performed traditional dances at the Topeka fairgrounds.

Traditional Potawatomi footwear.

By 1836, most of the Potawatomi had been forced onto reservations in land that would one day be the states of Oklahoma, Iowa, and Kansas. Some Potawatomi, however, hid in the woods of Wisconsin and Canada, while others stayed in Michigan, hiding themselves with their cousins, the Ottawa and Ojibwa. Today, the Potawatomi are spread across North American.

- The Prairie Band Potawatomi Nation lives in Kansas.
- The Citizen Potawatomi Nation is in Oklahoma
- The Forest County Potawatomi Community is in Wisconsin
- The Hannahville Indian Community is still in northern Michigan
- The Nattawaseppi Huron Band of Potawatomi lives in Athens, Michigan.
- The Pokagon Band of Potawatomi Indians lives in southern Michigan and in northern Indiana.

- The Walpole Island First Nation lives on an *unceded* island between the United States and Canada.

The Potawatomi who had been driven south into Kansas were forced to get used to the flat, empty prairies, a land that was very different from the forests and lakes of the Great Lakes region they had called home. At first, their reservation was a thirty-square-mile (78-square-kilometer) piece that included present-day Topeka. However, the Kansas–Nebraska Act of 1854 opened Kansas to settlers, and white *squatters* moved onto Potawatomi land.

The railroad brought yet another threat to the Potawatomi in Kansas, as did religious groups who were seeking to settle in the area. Still another danger came from within the tribe itself: 1,400 members of the tribe wanted to allow the U.S. government to divide their land into "allotments"—pieces of land that would belong to individuals rather than to the tribe as a whole—in exchange for the promise of becoming American

Nineteenth-century Potawatomi gathered to exchange goods and celebrate with spiritual dances.

With Liberty and Justice for All

When the United States was born in 1776, it was full of bright hopes. The new government used language that spoke of the rights and equality of "all men." But before the young nation could live up to its ideals, it would have to confront two issues—slavery and American Indians.

The U.S. government has a long history of struggling to handle the "Indian problem." Here is that history's timeline:

1787 Congress passes a law that promises Indian territories "shall never be taken from them without their consent and they shall never be invaded or disturbed, unless in just and lawful wars authorized by Congress."

1819 Congress passes the first appropriation of federal funds for Indians— $10,000 to be used to "civilize" them.

1824 Congress establishes the Bureau of Indian Affairs to supervise federal money spent on the various American Indian tribes.

1830 Indian Removal Act orders all Indians to move west of the Mississippi River.

1832 U.S. Supreme Court rules that Indians on reservations have immunity from state laws.

1887 Congress tries to break up the reservations by passing the Dawes Act, which gave each family 160 acres (65 hectares).

1890 Federal forces massacre about three hundred Lakota Sioux at Wounded Knee (the last battle between American Indians and federal forces).

1924 Congress declares all American Indians to be U.S. citizens.

1934 Congress reverses the Dawes Act and establishes new federally supervised tribal governments on the reservations.

1975 Congress passes the Indian Self-Determination and Education Assistance Act, which encourages maximum tribal participation in the government and education of their people.

1978 The Indian Child Welfare Act is passed, which maximizes tribal authority over child custody or adoption proceedings involving children who are tribal members or eligible for membership.

1988 Congress passes the Indian Gaming Regulatory Act, which opens the door to casinos on reservations.

citizens. These Potawatomi eventually left the group in Kansas—but 780 Potawatomi insisted on keeping their traditional **communal** ownership of the land. They were not interested in becoming citizens of the nation that had driven them from their homeland, and they refused to reject their cultural values. No single person could own the land, they firmly believed. This group became what is now the Prairie Band Potawatomi Nation.

Although the Potawatomi bands are now geographically separated, each year they come together in the fall for a Traditional Gathering. These gatherings give them the opportunity to share their cultural heritage and reaffirm their united identity.

After the railroad took 338,000 acres (136,784 hectares), the *Jesuits* 320 acres (130 hectares), and the Baptist church another 320,000 acres (129,500 hectares), the Potawatomi were left with only 77,357 acres (31,305 hectares). They settled down on their eleven-square-mile (28-square-kilometer) reservation, hoping to be left in peace.

In 1887, however, Congress passed the Dawes Act, also called the General Allotment Act. According to the U.S. government, it could no longer protect Indian lands from white settlement. Instead, it would divide up the reservations into family-sized farms and hand the pieces out to individual Indians. The government failed to understand the Indians' values; most Americans believed that it would be better for everyone—including the Indians themselves—if the various tribes were *assimilated* into American culture. Through the Dawes Act, the government hoped to end tribal relationships, including their relationship to the land.

The Potawatomi stubbornly refused to accept the land allotments. The U.S. government pressured them in a variety of ways: it withheld the payments due the Prairie Band; it gave double allotments to whites and members of other tribes who had accepted the Dawes Act; and it left only the poorest farming land to the Potawatomi.

The years that followed were desperate ones. The Prairie Band lived in poverty. They received little or no education, and they lacked any self-government. The U.S. government considered them to be *wards*; and it treated them like unwanted foster children.

Somehow, the Prairie Band weathered the difficult years from 1887 through the *Great Depression*. And then, slowly, things began to change in the United States. The Reorganization Act of 1934 finally put an end to the Dawes Act's allotment policy, and it returned surplus land to the Potawatomi. The Reorganization Act also sought to install a tribal government.

The Potawatomi Indian Agency building in the early twentieth century.

The Potawatomi were skeptical about this new government set in place by outsiders. All decisions made by the tribal government had to be approved by the Secretary of the Interior or the Commissioner of Indian Affairs. This meant that the tribe couldn't handle its own business ventures, money, or tribal decisions without first seeking approval from the U.S. bureaucrats. The new tribal government was based on the U.S. government's structure, rather than the Potawatomi's traditional "chief" concept. Few Potawatomi accepted this new government or its leaders.

The 1950s, known as the "Termination Period," brought still more jeopardy to the tribe. In 1954, the House of Representatives drafted a resolution that would withdraw federal recognition from five Indian tribes, including the Potawatomi. The Prairie Band sent petitions of protest to the federal government; it also sent **delegations** to Washington, D.C., to **lobby** for their tribe. Their united efforts saved them from termination.

Today, the Prairie Band Potawatomi Nation is alive and well. In the late twentieth century, the money generated by casinos brought a new surge of social, economic, educational, and cultural growth. As a result, the Prairie Band can now look to the future with hope.

Their present-day fortune, however, is rooted in their past. The Potawatomi remember the stories of their grandfathers—like the story of the last buffalo hunt—and they are inspired to keep alive their heritage of generosity and integrity.

The Prairie Band's government is working hard to ensure the future of these children.

Chapter Three

A Sovereign Nation: Potawatomi Government

Today, North American Indians have a unique place in the nations where they live. They are not considered an ethnic or racial minority group, the way many *immigrants* are; instead, as the very first Americans and Canadians, they have a special political status.

The members of the Prairie Band of Potawatomi, for example, are citizens of three *sovereigns*: their tribe, the United States of America, and the state of Kansas. In some ways, the United States relates to the Prairie Band—and to all federally recognized Indian nations—the way it would relate to another nation. The Prairie Band is like a small, independent country living within the boundaries of the United States. The U.S. government recognizes each tribal government's sovereignty.

The word *sovereignty* links together the concepts of both power and independence. Literally, the word means "unlimited power." A "sovereign"

The Prairie Band has its own emergency vehicles and police force.

has not merely been granted certain powers by a superior authority; instead, it is the independent source of its own power. The Prairie Band—and other American Indian nations—has *internal* sovereignty. This means it can make and enforce laws over its own people and land. When making and enforcing those laws, it answers only to its own people. Indian nations do not, however, have *external* sovereignty; in other words, they cannot interact with other governments independent of U.S. authority.

The states where reservations are located are sometimes reluctant to deal with Indian tribes as though they were equals, but the U.S. government has officially recognized their sovereignty since the United States was first formed. As we discussed in chapter two, U.S. policies often failed to honor tribal sovereignty, but more recently, every president since Richard Nixon has confirmed the government-to-government relationship that exists between tribal governments and the U.S. government. According to the Indian Self-Determination and Education Assistance Act, signed into law by President Gerald Ford in 1975, only congressional authority is higher than tribal authority—and state governance is generally not permitted within reservations.

The Prairie Band Nation's tribal seal.

A Sovereign Nation: Potawatomi Government   37

The government of the Prairie Band provides for all members of its nation, including senior citizens, who meet at this elder center.

The modern government of the Prairie Band Potawatomi Nation is a **democratic** one patterned in many ways after the U.S. government. Like the U.S. government, the Prairie Band has its own constitution that spells out the structure of its government. The elected government is the tribal council. It consists of seven individuals: the chair, vice chair, secretary, treasurer, and three other members. Their terms are staggered; for example, Zach Pahmahmie's term as chair expires in 2006, while Vice Chair Gary E. Mitchell's term expires in 2004.

Anyone in the Prairie Band can run for office, provided they have not been convicted of a **felony** within the past five years. Candidates for the offices of chairperson, vice chairperson, secretary, and treasurer must be at least twenty-five years old, while candidates for the office of council person need only be twenty-one years or older.

The council's main duties are to protect the health, peace, morals, education, and welfare of the tribe. According to the tribe's constitution, the tribal council also is responsible for protecting and preserving all tribal lands. The Prairie Band is determined to never again give up its land the way it was forced to do in the nineteenth century.

The constitution provides this list of the tribal council's other duties:

- Negotiate, consult, and contract with federal, state, local, and tribal governments, private enterprises, and individuals.
- Employ attorneys.
- Prevent any sale or lease of tribal land, funds, or assets without the consent of the tribe.
- Advise the Secretary of the Interior on federal funds appropriated to the Prairie Band.
- Govern future tribal membership, adoptions, and loss of membership.
- Regulate subordinate organizations and appoint committees.
- Enact laws and ordinances and take other actions to regulate law and order.
- Administer tribal elections.
- Regulate domestic relations.
- Administer the appointment and removal of subordinate tribal officials and employees.
- Prohibit trespass on tribal land.

The Prairie Band has its own law offices.

Preamble to the Prairie Band Potawatomi Nation's Constitution

We, the Prairie Band Potawatomi Nation, in order that our rights: inherit, United States Constitutional, treaty rights and other rights which arise from statutory law, Executive Order, tribal or other law and judicial administration be fully protected, exercised, and preserved, to insure justice and our security, to maintain Potawatomi traditions and customs, to promote harmony, the common good, social and general welfare and to secure the blessings of spiritual, educational, cultural, and economic development for ourselves and our posterity, do ordain and establish this constitution.

- Allocate funds for tribal land acquisition.
- Give special recognition to all veterans and members of the armed forces.
- Adopt and enforce zoning and land use codes.
- Make expenditures for tribal purposes.
- Levy and collect taxes.
- Protect the nation's natural resources, including water, air, timber, gas and oil, and other minerals.
- Regulate hunting, fishing, trapping, and plant gathering.
- Regulate public recreational activities.

The tribe's constitution also spells out what it means to be a member of the Prairie Band. Today's membership requirements specify that a person must be at least one quarter Indian and be blood descendents of the original Prairie Band land allottees.

The Potawatomi Tribal Gaming Commission is another part of the Prairie Band's tribal government. It is made up of five members who are elected by the tribal council to serve four-year terms. The Gaming Commission regulates the tribe's casino and any other gaming enterprises. It also issues gaming licenses and is responsible for ensuring that all gaming employees undergo background investigations. The commission's task is to make sure that all gaming activities promote the tribe's economic development and self-sufficiency. It also acts to shield the Prairie Band Nation from organized crime.

The revenue generated by the Prairie Band's casino has made a tremendous difference to many areas of life on the reservation. For example, in 1999, a new 1.5 million-dollar tribal government building was completed—paid for completely by funds from the casino. The new government center houses several tribal programs; more than eighty employees work there.

The Prairie Band Nation has also recently built its own police department building. The Jackson County Sheriff's Department once handled emergency situations and crimes that took place on the reservation. But in 1996, the nation received a grant from the U.S. Justice Department and the Bureau of Indian Affairs for the development of a tribal police department. The department now has an officer and a dispatcher on duty at all times. This means that the tribe has the authority to make and enforce its laws.

The Potawatomi Tribal Court also has an important role in the Prairie Band's government. The Tribal District Court judge conducts hearings and trials, while the Tribal Court of Appeals has three judges who hear appeals from trial court decisions. All these judges are licensed attorneys—and they are American Indians who are familiar with both federal and state law *and* Potawatomi history and tradition.

The Prairie Band Tribal Court's **jurisdiction** covers the people and activities on the reservation. In **civil** cases, the court's authority is greater than the state's, even when non-Indians are involved (so long as the case arose within the reservation's boundaries). What's more, the Tribal Court has **exclusive** jurisdiction over all cases that involve Potawatomi children. Even if a juvenile case arises in courts outside the reservation, the Federal Indian Child Welfare Act gives tribal courts the right to assume jurisdiction.

The modern government of the Prairie Band Potawatomi is very different from the traditional government that centered on a chief. In the mid-twentieth century, the tribe went through a difficult period of adjustment as it learned to work with a strange and unwelcome system. Today, however, the Prairie Band has a proud and independent government that seeks to govern with wisdom and justice. Funded by the new revenue from Indian gaming, the government is guiding its people into more prosperous living conditions—while still holding on to traditional Potawatomi values.

Many Potawatomi are Christians.

Chapter 4

The Spiritual World: Potawatomi Religion

Religion is often a very private thing. Although we usually gather with groups of "believers," people who think and feel the same way we do about God and the spiritual world, we are often uncomfortable discussing our spiritual practices with those who do not share our beliefs. We are afraid we may be misunderstood; we suspect that others may cast doubt on our religion; and ultimately, we do not want to risk exposing something so private and so important to our innermost being.

Many North American Indians feel the same way about their religion. They are not comfortable revealing the details of their spiritual practices to outsiders—and they have good reason to fear that others may try to diminish the importance of their beliefs. After all, for centuries the government and *missionary* groups tried to wipe out Native religions. For many years, some Native spiritual practices were even illegal in the United States.

Native religions experience a deep sense of connection to the Earth.

Christian groups considered Indian spirituality to be "heathen" or evil. Then, in the twentieth century, **New Agers** were attracted to Native religions; these people adopted many Native practices without fully grasping their deep meaning. Native religious ceremonies became a fad—but many North American Indians thought these New Age ceremonies were disrespectful, if not sacrilegious.

As outsiders, we can never truly comprehend the religious beliefs of another group. We can only crane our necks to catch a glimpse of something that lies outside our experience. If we keep our minds open and respectful, however, we may find that our understanding of our own spiritual beliefs are enriched and widened.

For many Christian Americans, religion is a once-in-awhile sort of thing. They may go to church on Sundays or celebrate the major religious holidays (like Christmas and Easter), but they seldom think about the spiritual world in between these events. The Potawatomi, however, see religion very differently.

Traditionally, the Potawatomi do not practice religion only on certain days. Instead, their religion is an all-the-time way of living. It puts them in contact with the spiritual world day by day and moment by moment. The Potawatomi do have special ceremonies, however, that help them to live out this daily religion. One of the most important of these is the Drum Dance.

The Drum Dance combines some of the fundamental parts of Christianity (for instance, the central role of Christ) with Native traditions. Christ is **personified** in the Drum Dance. The Dance speaks to all areas of Potawatomi life—right and wrong, physical and spiritual healing, love and death—and it has power over all the important turning points in life, like birth, naming, marriage, and burial.

Spirituality adds meaning and dignity to the lives of many Potawatomi.

The Drum Dance may have grown from the Potawatomi's ancient roots—the Ojibwa/Chippewa also practiced a very similar ceremony—but the Dance did not become popular among the Prairie Band until the late nineteenth century. Through the early twentieth century, it grew in importance. Other nearby tribes, like the Fox, the Kickapoo, and the Osage, also practiced a similar ceremony.

In Ruth Landes' book *The Prairie Potawatomi: Tradition and Ritual in the Twentieth Century*, she describes the information she gained about the Drum Dance from talking with a Potawatomi named Topash, a drummer who represented "Thunder." During a summer of terrible drought, Topash used his position to bring rain to the reservation. He told Landes what happened:

The summer of 1930 was pretty dry. We were having the mid-summer dance the whites call the Corn Dance. It was quite hot and the head brave could have sung for rain, but he didn't. So I and my assistant took it up, laying out Indian tobacco and singing for a good shower. . . . We

The Potawatomi reveal their sense of order and harmony in their traditional artwork.

The Potawatomi often feel that their spirituality roots them in the Earth, as this Native artist portrays in a work titled Root Think.

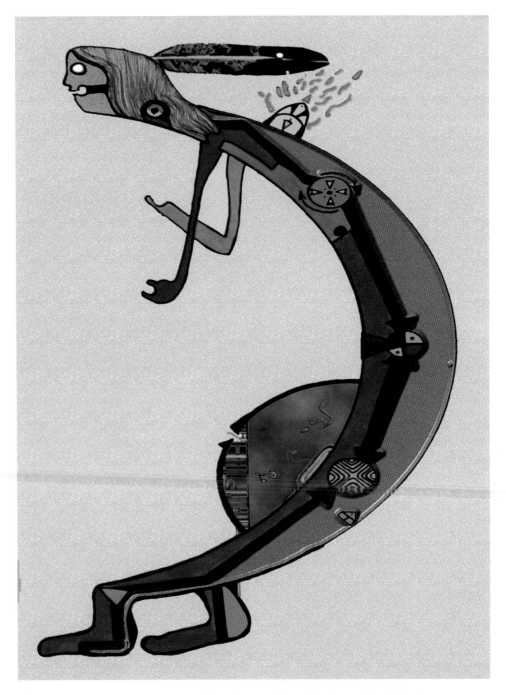

This painting portrays a Native artist's image of an effective spiritual leader—someone who is attuned to the small cycles of nature and life, who moves softly and carries the good faith of his people with him in his mysterious and difficult work.

In the past, the Drum Dance was a distinct and separate religious practice, but today, many Potawatomi combine it with the religious practices of the Native American Church. This religion varies across North America, but in general, like the Drum Dance, it combines aspects of Christianity with traditional Native beliefs; *peyote*, however, is the Native American Chruch's central *sacrament*. In 1925, the Native North American Church of God was *chartered* in Kansas; twenty-first-century Potawatomi may take part in its services along with the Drum Dance, without feeling any conflict of interests.

Not all Potawatomi participate in either the Drum Dance or the Native American Church, of course. Many are Christians who belong to one of a number of churches—Catholic, Baptist, and Methodist, and others. Even those who are Christian, however, often feel perfectly comfortable participating in the Drum Dance *and* going to church. Most *fundamentalist* Christians are convinced that God would not condone the Drum Dance—but Potawatomi often feel that the Creator ignores the boundary lines between religions. The Drum Dance and the Native American Church offer the Potawatomi a way to resist being swallowed by the mainstream culture of America; these spiritual practices allow the Potawatomi to worship God (and even Christ) while remaining rooted in their cultural identity.

Children once learned who they were from their clan. Today, the tribal government provides a new sense of social structure.

Chapter 5

Depending on One Another: Potawatomi Social Structures

Imagine that you belong to a huge family where your grandparents and even great-grandparents live with you and help raise you; your cousins are as close to you as your brothers and sisters; and your aunts and uncles are another set of parents who watch out for you and teach you about life. After you were born, you were given a special name that connected you both to God and to your enormous family. Your name makes you feel special, because it is more than just a label; it tells you who you are; it connects you to your family; and it gives you power. No matter what life brings, you know you will always be able to rely on your family to watch out for you and care for you. You will never ever be alone.

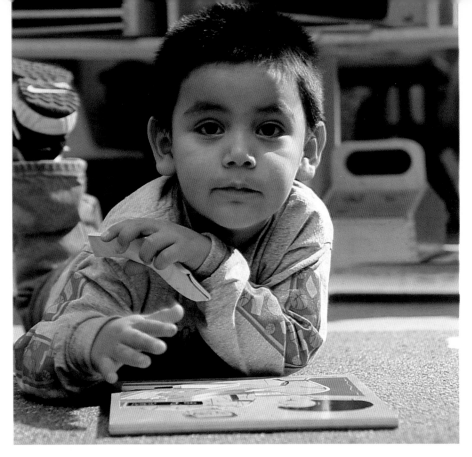

This little boy is growing up to a brighter tomorrow, thanks to the hard work of the Prairie Band Potawatomi Nation.

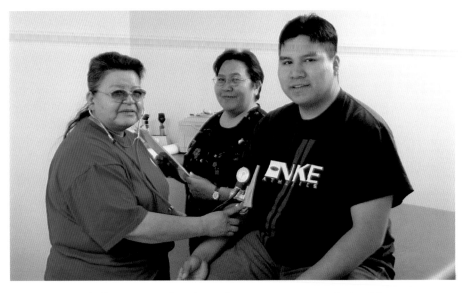

Tribal nurses work to keep the Potawatomi people healthy.

If you're like the majority of North Americans, your life is very different from this description. You probably live with your parents—or with one of your parents—and your brothers and sisters. You may talk to your grandparents on the phone or have dinner with them once in a while—or they may live far away and visit only at Christmas or on other special occasions. You may feel close to some of your aunts and uncles and cousins, but others you barely know, and your families only get together occasionally. You like your name all right, but you never think much about what it means; it's just the label that people use to refer to you. When you grow up, you plan to head into the world on your own. You look forward to being independent; maybe you can't wait to get away from your family and be your own person. As much as you love your parents—and you know they love you—once you graduate and get a job, you know it's up to you to support yourself in life.

These are two very different ways of looking at life. For centuries, the Potawatomi lived in clans, a system that resembled the enormous family de-

A powwow offers the opportunity to get together with others and share good times.

Depending on One Another   55

The Prairie Band provides food assistance to those in need.

scribed above—but North American culture has gradually broken down the strength of the clan structure. Like all North Americans, some Potawatomi move across the country, looking for better jobs. In today's world, it is often hard to maintain close connections between clan members.

Without a strong clan system, however, Native Americans are more vulnerable to the negative forces of our society—substance abuse, poverty, family violence, suicide—while at the same time, they often lack the economic and educational resources that other North American groups may enjoy. The Prairie Band is working hard to build a tribal system that supports all its members the way the clans once did. With the revenue generated by its gaming enterprises, the tribe is building successful social programs to address its members' needs.

The Prairie Band Alcohol and Drug Program, for instance, provides individual counseling, outreach programs, referrals, and post-treatment guidance to those who struggle with addiction. Parr Ranch is a tribal program for recovering alcoholics; it works as a stepping-stone from addiction to a productive life. Alcoholics Anonymous and church services are part of this

The tribal council oversees housing programs.

program, and so are traditional healing ceremonies, such as **sweats**, **pow-wows**, and Drum Dances.

The tribe is also working to take care of its young people. The Traditional Parenting Class helps parents take advantage of their cultural strengths while they learn about modern child development practices. The Prairie Band also received from **HUD** a $685,000 grant that allowed them to build the Ben-no-tteh ("child's house" in Potawatomi) Wigwam, which houses the Early Childhood Program. The Johnson O'Malley Program provides tutoring to school-age children; it also looks for ways to get Potawatomi culture into the schoolroom through art, music, literature, history projects, field trips, and guest speakers. The Boys & Girls' Club is also active on the Potawatomi reservation. It works to improve and maintain young people's spiritual, physical, mental, and emotional well-being through sports, education, parent involvement, and Potawatomi traditions.

The tribe also has many programs for adults, including adult education

The older generation still has much to offer those who are younger.

The nation provides counseling and other programs for alcoholics.

Some Potawatomi Clans

Thunder	Bear	Elk
Fish	Beaver	Wolf
Eagle	Coyote	Warrior
Brave	Angel	Sun
Moon	Blackbird	Pheasant
Duck	Silver Fox	

Clan membership is inherited through the father.

programs, vocational training, and scholarship programs. Many other programs perform other services:

- The Employee Assistance Program helps tribal employees with personal, family, or job problems.
- The Community Health Program provides medical home visits, blood pressure screening, and referrals to other health facilities.
- The Elder Center delivers meals to homebound senior citizens, helps older people buy groceries, and provides sixty to seventy

Boys & Girls Clubs offer sports and other activities to young people on the Prairie Band Reservation.

New paved roads are improving life on the reservation.

meals a week at a center where senior citizens can eat and social-
ize.
- The Food Distribution/Commodity Program helps people (both Indian and non-Indian) who are in need of emergency food service.
- The Housing Authority works to provide tribal members with affordable housing.
- Social Services works to promote family unity and self-sufficiency.
Its services include individual counseling, crisis intervention, financial assistance, and alternate resource development.

The Prairie Band's value statement commits the tribe to promoting the
"health, safety, and quality of life for all." Through its many programs, it is
living out this commitment. The clan system may no longer provide the vi-
tal social structure that it once did—but the members of the Prairie Band
Potawatomi Nation still know they can always depend on one another.

Potawatomi artistry is demonstrated in traditional clothing.

Chapter 6

A Creative People;
Potawatomi Arts

Whative People; Marty Kreipe de Montano graduated from the University of Kansas with her master's degree, she soon realized she would find no jobs back home on the Prairie Band Reservation. Her degree was in special studies, similar to a museum studies degree, so she left her home behind and headed for New York City where museum jobs were far more plentiful.

She got a job with the George Hye Foundation, and she and her daughter Molly found a place to live on the edge of Harlem. It wasn't easy for them to get used to their new home. New York City was very different from the Kansas prairies. The people seemed rude and pushy to Marty, and they always seemed to be in such a hurry. She wasn't used to everyone walking so fast!

But Marty enjoyed her work at the Hye Foundation. Far away from her home and her people, she found herself gaining a new awareness of her

Even everyday objects become works of art.

own people's art and creativity. She had the opportunity to work with a vast collection of artwork that included Native objects from Alaska to South America. Best of all, the Hye Foundation had over seven hundred pieces of Potawatomi work—wooden bowls and spoons, beaded vests and other beadwork, and medicine bags. Marty was impressed by the incredible variety of her own culture.

The founder of the Hye Foundation, George Hye, had traveled across North America during the Great Depression buying Native artwork. He often read the newspaper obituaries to find out when someone who owned an Indian collection had died, and then he was sure to put in an offer before anyone else could. Early in the twentieth century, a man named M. R. Harrington worked for Hye, and Harrington was the one who traveled through Kansas and purchased most of Hye's collection of Potawatomi art.

The Potawatomi are skilled in fabric arts.

Beadwork adds beauty to a traditional bag.

Recently, Marty Kreipe de Montano came back to the reservation in Kansas. She was there for a very special reason—she was signing copies of a book she had written. She was amazed and delighted to find long lines of her own people waiting for their autographed copy of *Coyote in Love with a Star.* "It was more than I expected," she told the Prairie Band's Web site.

Marty's book is a fanciful sort of autobiography. It tells the adventures of Coyote, who leaves the wide, flat Potawatomi reservation in Kansas and travels to New York City in search of work. When he reaches the big city, he finds a job as a Rodent Control Officer in the World Trade Center. Far away from his home, he grows lonely and homesick, so at the end of each day, he escapes New York's bustling crowds by climbing to the top of the tall building. There, he looks up at the night sky and discovers the most beautiful star he has ever seen. Marty used this simple story to give readers information and images about Native culture. She also included a glossary of words in different Indian languages.

Now that New York has changed since September 11, 2001, and the

World Trade Center is gone, Marty plans to write a new story that will reflect the city's changes. She comes from a long line of creative people, and she is eager to express her own creativity through her writing.

Although Marty makes her home in New York City, she still loves the reservation where she grew up. When she went back to her old home, she was impressed by all the changes. The dirt roads she remembered were now smooth and paved; the feeling of despair had changed to one of hope. "It's a different atmosphere here now," she told the Prairie Band's news Web site, "with so many people employed and money going into the *infrastructure*."

Like Marty, many Potawatomi have settled away from the reservation. Jack Wooldridge, a Potawatomi author and illustrator, was born on the Cit-

A traditional bandolier bag.

A Creative People: Potawatomi Arts   67

izen Potawatomi Nation Reservation in Shawnee, Oklahoma, but he now makes his home in Santa Cruz, California. Although Jack was born on the reservation, he was raised non-Indian; as an adult, however, he has come to appreciate his cultural heritage. His Potawatomi roots give him a sense of direct connection to the Earth.

Jack wrote and illustrated the Potawatomi Fable Series. He illustrates other children's stories as well, and he has worked with publishers like McGraw-Hill to develop educational materials. Now he is working on a story translated from English into the Potawatomi language.

Although Marty de Montano and Jack Wooldrige have left their reservations, their homelands still call them back. Each year, Jack returns to the Citizen Potawatomi Nation for the Heritage Festival Days. And one day, Marty hopes to retire to the Prairie Band's reservation in Kansas. She

The Potawatomi are skilled at beadwork.

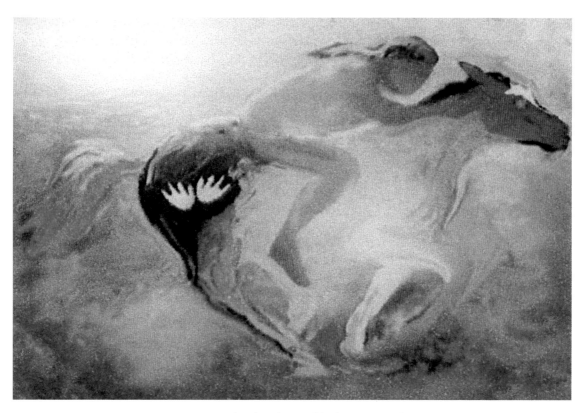

An example of Jack Wooldridge's artwork.

would like to watch her grandchildren grow up there. Far away from the hurry and noise of New York City, she plans to simply sit in her backyard and reflect on the meaning of life.

People like Marty Kreipe de Montano and Jack Wooldridge are good representatives of their people. Their work is enjoyed across North America, educating others about the Potawatomi culture. And they are keeping alive the Potawatomi's heritage of creativity.

The Potawatomi are a generous people who reach out to those in need.

Chapter 7

A Habit of Generosity: Contributions to Society

"It is a time not to forget the past but to build on it," says *The Prairie Band Potawatomi: Chapters in Time*. Much has changed for twenty-first-century Potawatomi people, but despite all the changes, the Prairie Band is trying to live their lives according to their ancestors' values.

A hundred years ago, the Potawatomi hunting party gave half their buffalo to help a community in trouble. Today, the Prairie Band continues this spirit of generosity. Gaming enterprises have brought new economic hope to the reservation—and the tribe is sharing their good fortune with those around them. The Prairie Band is dedicated to doing what they can for the well-being of their neighbors, both on and off the reservation. As a result,

The Potawatomi share their culture with the rest of the world at powwows.

they not only care for their own people but they also donate funds to others in need.

You might think the Potawatomi have good reason to be bitter. The U.S. government has a long history of broken promises; as a result the Prairie Band makes its home far from their original homeland in the Great Lakes region. But the tribe believes that their success depends in part on letting go of their resentment so that they can develop strong relationships with the communities around them. According to the Prairie Band's Web site:

> Following decades of poverty and geographic isolation on our reservation, Indian gaming offers a unique opportunity to speak our concerns

with strong voices. By nurturing connections with outside communities through our numerous goodwill efforts and contributions, many non-Indians now better understand and support our struggle for sovereignty. . . .

Prairie Band member Gary Mitchell is pleased by the funds his tribe has donated to the local school district. He says the donation "gives the nation the opportunity to pay its own way in the field of education for its youth and to lessen dependence on others."

John Rundel, superintendent of the local school district, is grateful for the tribe's generosity. The contribution came just when it was needed most, he says. "It allowed us to maintain programming we might have had to do without under other circumstances." Because of the Potawatomi donation, athletic programs could be expanded. "The generosity of [the Prairie Band] certainly emphasizes their concern and interest in all youth."

Reaching Out

After the terrorist attacks of September 11, 2001, the Prairie Band Potawatomi Nation felt the need to do what they could to help the rescue and relief efforts in New York City and Washington, D.C. So they donated $100,000 to the Red Cross. "It's a drop in the bucket compared to what is needed," said tribal chairman Badger Wahwasuck, but hopefully it can help people. Our tribe gives its condolences to all the families and especially to the rescue workers, firefighters and police officers."

Earlier that same year, the Prairie Band gave $50,000 to the Red Cross to help the tornado victims in Hoisington, Kansas. Chairman Wahwasuck said of his tribe's gift, "We were fortunate to be in a position to help those in need; we're confident we could count on the residents of Kansas to assist us in a time of need. It's important to support unity and to sustain a far-reaching network of family and friends."

Gaming allows the Potawatomi to give to those in need.

The Prairie Band's Web site concludes:

Charitable contributions made possible by gaming offer an opportunity for us to grow forward from our rich and colorful history—collecting strength and understanding along the way. It challenges us to reach out: Encourage public support for Indian self-reliance and secure a promising future for all by continuing to support charitable giving.

When the Prairie Band submitted to the Bureau of Indian Affairs their outline for gaming expenditures, they proposed that one percent of all their gaming revenues would be donated to charitable organizations. Their proposal was approved by the Bureau of Indian Affairs and the tribe's general council. Their generous contributions have given them positive newspaper

Potawatomi Charitable Donations

In 2001, the Prairie Band Potawatomi Nation donated nearly a million dollars to local school districts and numerous nonprofit organizations. Here are some of the organizations that received funds from the Prairie Band:

Royal Valley School District	$200,000
American Red Cross (9/11 relief)	$100,000
Kickapoo Nation School	$100,000
Let's Help, Inc.	$100,000
Battered Women Taskforce	$50,000
Hoisington Tornado Relief	$50,000
Topeka Rescue Mission	$50,000
Topeka Public Schools	$50,000
Topeka High School (band uniforms)	$6,730
Topeka Youth Project	$1,000

The Generosity of North American Indians

The Potawatomi are not the only Indian nation committed to a spirit of generosity. According to a survey taken by the National Indian Gaming Association, every year U.S. Indian nations give at least 68 million dollars in charitable donations. About 80 percent of these donations go to local or community efforts; non-Indian organizations receive 38 percent of the donations.

The older generation has a heritage of wisdom that enriches the present-day world.

Tribally owned gas stations contribute to the Prairie Band's prosperity.

and television coverage. The best public relations, the Potawatomi believe, come from building bridges between themselves and the rest of the world.

Native Americans have always understood that creation is an interconnected web of life. What strengthens one strand will ultimately strengthen all the web—and what weakens one strand will in the end damage the web's entire structure. The Potawatomi are working for the future by building the strands that connect them to the world around them. In the end, they know that their nation will be improved—and so will our entire world.

The Prairie Band Potawatomi have great hopes for their children's future.

Chapter 8

Hopes for the Future, Challenges for Today

Imagine that aliens from another planet landed on Earth. These aliens worked hard to destroy the language we on Earth had always spoken, and eventually they succeeded; soon all the children being born on Earth could only speak the aliens' language. Only the old people remembered the languages we spoke before the aliens came. Now imagine trying to hold a church service, throw a birthday party, sing Christmas carols, or share your grandparents' memories. You wouldn't be able to, not if you had forgotten the language. And so, gradually, society on Earth would change. We would no longer have words for the things we once considered important, and we would stop thinking about them. Our connection to our history would be erased; we would lose huge chunks of our music, our literature, our folklore, and even our jokes. Eventually, our society would merge with the aliens' culture—and all that we had once been would be lost.

Older people share their language with the younger generation.

That is what is happening to North American Indians. The Potawatomi hope to save their language before it is too late. But it will not be easy.

Eddie Joe Mitchell, Mary Wabnum, and Mary LeClere are three young people who are determined to hold on to one of their most valuable possessions—their native language. Together with other Potawatomi young people, they worked to start their own language class.

One man in their tribe laughed at them. "You can't learn to talk Potawatomi," he said. And when the group asked **linguists** to help them, their requests were denied or ignored. But Eddie Joe Mitchell and the others did not give up. They decided they would make the class happen without any outside help; they didn't even ask for financial assistance.

Potawatomi elders wanted to save their language, and they volunteered to help the language class. Older Potawatomi, like Nelson Potts and Irving Shopteese, Cecilia "Meeks" Jackson and Alberta "Shaw no que" Wamego, taught the classes. These older people asked for nothing in return for their time.

Fifty to sixty students eventually attended the class at one time or another, but only Eddie Joe Mitchell, Mary Wabnum, and Mary LeClere stuck with it. Today they have learned about six thousand Potawatomi words, and they can put them together into sentences. They are not discouraged that they are the only ones to have **persevered** in the study of the language, because they know that if three people can learn the language, those three can each teach another three, and then those nine will each teach three

Younger Potawatomi have the opportunity to experience their cultural heritage.

Potawatomi children learn about their culture.

more people . . . and ripples of strength and renewal will spread through the entire tribe. "The obligation of the students is to pass on what they have learned to another generation of Potawatomi," said Eddie Joe.

The loss of language is not the only challenge confronting the Potawatomi. As they enter the twenty-first century, they must face many problems.

Poverty and alcoholism continue to be major issues to overcome. The lack of housing, jobs, and education are often components of these issues. The Prairie Band sees economic development as one answer. It defines economic growth as:

- increased employment
- increased average income
- improved overall quality of life

The Prairie Band has set itself goals for the future. Its twenty-year plan defines the overall goals as being: "the development of resources, leading to a higher standard of living, increased cultural vitality and greater freedom to make choices concerning the Potawatomi future." The nation's short-term goals include:

- road improvements
- housing plans
- education
- improved utility and phone systems

The Prairie Band fire station does its part to keep the Potawatomi people safe.

We Are a Living People

I don't understand.
Why should anyone's identity be defined by your games?
We are a living people.
Why are we used as entertainment for schools?
We are a living people.
Why must we be used as nicknames, logos, and mascots?
We are a living people.
Why must we, a living people, be singled out?
Why must we, a living people, be stereotyped?
. . . Why do you treat US, a living people, as relics?
Why is OUR culture for sale?
. . . Respect should be such a simple thing!
Why do YOU make it so hard?
Why do WE make it so hard?

By Lori Wautier (tribal member and high school student), read at
Wisconsin Senate Education Committee hearing on SB217 on
March 15, 2000.

They plan to use the revenue generated by gaming enterprises to bring these goals into reality.

Not all tribal members, however, are happy about the casinos and other gambling that has come to their land. Some feel gambling is immoral, and they do not like profiting from it; others worry that it will bring crime to their community.

Like all human beings, the Potawatomi do not always agree on the best way to do things. But they are working to resolve their differences. They are also working toward a greater harmony with non-Indians.

This is not always easy. Native groups across North America struggle against the racism that is often imbedded in our society. Many North

Casinos and other gaming activities are helping to change the future of the Potawatomi.

Prairie Band Potawatomi Nation's Tribal Vision Statement

As a sovereign Nation, we shall ensure self-sufficiency that respects diversity and equality while working within a spirit of cooperation and fairness for a high standard of living and quality of life.

As a sovereign Nation we shall strive to provide an environment of improved well-being for our people, including education, health, safety, and welfare, while valuing our culture, traditions, and all resources.

As a sovereign Nation we shall accomplish this for all generations with a system of value-based management to respect all views.

New roads are one of the Prairie Band's goals for the future.

Americans do not even realize that their attitudes and language are demeaning to Native people.

For example, many schools athletic teams use **mascots** borrowed from American Indian cultures—sacred objects, ceremonial traditions and dress, and words—without understanding their deep meaning or appropriate use. Cartoons, toys, and other children's media often portray Indians inappropriately as well. All of these things help to promote and maintain stereotypes.

The Potawatomi people are far different from what they were a hundred years ago, or even twenty years. They have worked hard to bring a new

Powwows celebrate Native Americans' past, present, and future.

As the Potawatomi move into the twenty-first century, they appreciate the importance of working together. This Native painting titled Collaboration represents the importance of breathing and working together as one.

"The fight to eliminate Indian nicknames and images in sports is only one front of the larger battle to eliminate obstacles that confront American Indians. . . . They are particularly inappropriate and insensitive in light of the long history of forced assimilation that American Indian people have endured in this country."

prosperity and well-being to their communities. As they struggle to hold on to their culture and language, they are reaching out to the world around them, changing the way non-Indians perceive them. There is still work to be done—but they are facing the future with hope and strength.

The Potawatomi's creative heritage helps to keep them grounded in traditional values as they enter the twenty-first century.

American Indian Facts

- 16 percent of Indian males and 13 percent of Indian females sixteen years and older are unemployed, compared with the percent national average.
- The suicide rate for fifteen- to twenty-four-year-old Indians is more than twice that of any other ethnic group.
- Indians die younger than other population groups—13 percent of Indian deaths occur under age twenty-five, compared with the percent national average.
- The alcoholism rate for fifteen- to twenty-four-year-old Indians is more than seventeen times the national average.
- Homicide is the second leading cause of death among Indians fourteen years and younger, and the third leading cause of death for Indians fifteen to twenty-four years old.
- 66 percent of American Indians twenty-five years old and older have at least a high school diploma, compared with the national average of 75 percent.
- About nine percent of American Indians have completed at least a bachelor's degree, compared with the 20-percent national average.
- 31 percent of American Indians live below the national poverty level, compared to a national poverty rate of approximately 13 percent.

Source: North Carolina Commission on Indian Affairs

Further Reading

Clifton, James A. *The Potawatomi*. New York: Chelsea House, 1987.

Clifton, James A. *The Prairie People*. Iowa City: University of Iowa Press, 1998.

Cornell, George and Gordon Henry. *Ojibwa*. Philadelphia: Mason Crest, 2004.

Greene, Jacqueline D. *The Chippewa*. New York: Franklin Watts, 1993.

Powell, Suzanne. *The Potawatomi*. New York: Franklin Watts, 1997.

Whelan, Gloria. *Night of the Full Moon*. New York: Knopf, 1993.

For More Information

Citizen Potawatomi Nation
thorpe.ou.edu

Pokagon Band of Potawatomi Indians
www.pokagon.com

Potawatomi Stories
www.ukans.edu/~kansite/pbp/books/mitch

Potawatomi Web
www.ukans.edu/~kansite/pbp/people/home.html

Prairie Band Potawatomi Nation
www.pbpindiantribe.com

Publisher's Note:

The Web sites listed on this page were active at the time of publication. The publisher is not responsible for Web sites that have changed their address or discontinued operation since the date of publication. The publisher will review and update the Web sites upon each reprint.

Glossary

assimilated: Made to take on the characteristics of another culture so they can "fit in."

chartered: Granted rights, privileges, or franchises from the sovereign power.

civil: Relating to private rights and remedies sought by action or suit.

communal: Characterized by group ownership and participation.

delegations: Groups of people chosen to represent others.

democratic: Government of the people based on the principles of equality.

exclusive: Excluding others from participation.

fast: To go without food.

felony: A serious crime declared so due to the possible punishment.

fundamentalist: Someone who believes in the strict interpretation of the Bible.

Great Depression: A period of low wages and high unemployment beginning in 1929 and lasting until about 1939.

HUD: Housing and Urban Development. A federal agency whose responsibilities include providing affordable housing for low-income people.

immigrants: A person who comes to this country to establish residence.

Indian agent: An official representative of the federal government to American Indian tribes.

infrastructure: The system of public works, including roads and utility systems, for a region, city, or state.

invasive: Tending to spread.

Jesuits: Members of the Roman Catholic Society of Jesus.

jurisdiction: The power, right, or authority to interpret and apply the law.

linguists: People who are accomplished in languages, often speaking several languages.

lobby: To try to influence others, often government representatives.

mascots: People, animals, or objects adopted by a group (often an athletic team) as a symbol, usually for luck.

missionary: A person who undertakes the ministry of spreading a religion.

New Agers: People who participate in the social movement of the late 20th century that drew from ancient concepts, especially Eastern and American traditions.

persevered: Persisted, kept trying.

personified: Represented a person; to have human characteristics.

peyote: A spineless cactus.

pictographs: Drawings or paintings on a rock wall.

powwows: Social gatherings and celebrations of culture, often with many tribes participating, where arts and crafts are exhibited and sold and traditional dances can be observed.

reservation: Public land put aside by the federal government for use by American Indians.

sacrament: A religious rite or observance.

sovereigns: People with supreme power.

squatters: People who settle on property without right, title, or payment of rent.

sweats: A type of purification rite.

unceded: Not given away.

value system: The principles or qualities in which people believe.

wards: People under guard, protection, or supervision, usually from an agency.

Western: Having to do with the culture of the United States and Western Europe.

Index

Biographies

Martha McCollough received her bachelor's and master's degrees in anthropology at the University of Alaska-Fairbanks, and she now teaches at the University of Nebraska. Her areas of study are contemporary Native American issues, ethnohistory, and the political and economic issues that surround encounters between North American Indians and Euroamericans.

Ellyn Sanna has authored more than eighty books for educational and inspirational publishers. She is also an editor who works in upstate New York, where she lives with her husband and three children—and their cat, rabbit, two hamsters, and many fish.